Internet Invention

David Glover

Ginn

Telephone + Computer = Internet

Today we take the Internet for granted. We send e-mails, look up web sites to help with homework, download music, watch the latest movie trailers, and chat to friends online. But how did the Internet start? Who invented it? How does it work?

Two incredible inventions made the Internet possible – the telephone and the computer. On their own, the telephone and the computer would make most peoples' **top-ten** of great inventions. Together, they are changing the world into a **'global village'**.

As you meet the inventors who helped create the Internet, write down and keep your answers to each QUIZ question. (Remember, the answers are in the book!) World Wide Web, here we come!

Inventing the Inventions

The Telephone

Alexander Graham Bell invented the telephone in 1876.

PAGES 6 TO 11

The Computer

Charles Babbage designed the first computer in the 1830s.

PAGES 12 TO 17

The Microchip

Take a look inside the inventions ...

PAGES **18** TO **19**

The Internet

In 1973, Bob Kahn and Vinton Cerf invented the Internet.

PAGES **20** TO **31**

The Telephone

HOT NEWS … On 25th October 1854, W. H. Russell, a reporter for *The Times* newspaper, witnessed the charge of the Light Brigade at the Battle of Balaclava. But his report did not reach London for more than two weeks. With no telephones or radios to send instant news from war zones, Russell's report travelled overland on horseback and across water by ship.

Samuel Morse

Lived	1791–1872
Born	Charlestown, USA
Job	Painter and inventor

The Morse code

A .-	H	O ---	V ...-
B -...	I ..	P .--.	W .--
C -.-.	J .---	Q --.-	X -..-
D -..	K -.-	R .-.	Y -.--
E .	L .-..	S ...	Z --..
F ..-.	M --	T -	
G --.	N -.	U ..-	

But things were about to change. Telegraph wires had started to spread like spiders' webs and by 1866 a cable had been laid under the Atlantic Ocean between Britain and America. Why? In 1834, Samuel Morse had invented the telegraph. With a simple code of dots and dashes, it sent messages along wires stretched between telegraph poles or buried underground.

An early Morse telegraph

To send a telegraph message you had to visit a telegraph office, where an operator tapped out your message. You had to pay for every character, so people kept their messages short – just like text messages today. At the other end of the line, a telegraph clerk wrote the message on a slip of paper, and handed it to a telegraph boy. The telegraph boy would then run, or cycle, to the delivery address, hand over the message and wait for any reply (and a tip!).

Alexander Graham Bell

Lived	1847–1922
Born	Edinburgh, Scotland
Job	Hearing specialist and inventor

But, all this was about to change. Why? In 1876, Alexander Graham Bell invented the telephone. Instant communication had arrived. Once people realised they could talk directly over long distances, they all wanted telephones in their homes. **It's good to talk!**

Let's Get Technical

A basic telephone has a mouthpiece and an earpiece. The mouthpiece changes the sound of your voice into an electric signal with the same pattern, and sends it down the telephone line. The earpiece changes the electric signal it receives back into the sound of your voice.

Today you can phone anyone in the world. Nearly every home in Britain has at least one telephone. Telephone signals are carried by electricity along wires, by light along optical fibres and by radio waves through the air. But if you phone a relative in India or Australia, your conversation bounces from a satellite in space, thousands of miles above Earth's surface!

FIBRE FACT

A single optical fibre, which is about the thickness of a human hair, can carry the equivalent of 300 million telephone calls at the same time! That's roughly all the phone calls going on in America at any one time.

Blah Blah Blah Blah Blah Blah Blah Blah Blah Blah Blah Blah Blah Blah

A mobile phone sends and receives calls using invisible microwaves.

The Computer

In 1642, the French mathematician Blaise Pascal built a machine to help his father with his work. Pascal's father was a tax collector and his son's machine was the first successful calculator. It did not use electricity like a modern calculator – it worked with levers and gear wheels, like a clock.

Blaise Pascal

Lived	1623–1662
Born	Clermont-Ferrand, France
Job	Mathematician, scientist and writer

Other inventors improved his ideas, and then, in the 1830s, Charles Babbage designed a machine that could be 'programmed' to do any kind of calculation. He called his invention the 'Analytical Engine'. **It was the first computer!**

Charles Babbage

Lived   1791–1871
Born   London, England
Job   Mathematician and inventor

Pascal's calculator

13

During the Second World War, German forces used complicated codes to send secret messages. Can you break a code? You can if you find the 'key' used to swap one letter for another. But the only way for British code-breakers to read the secret messages was to try millions of different keys, one at a time. **At first it seemed impossible!** But with the help of the first computers, the codes were broken. The man behind these code-breaking computers (the starting point for all computers ever invented since!) was the mathematician Alan Turing.

Alan Turing

Lived	1912–1954
Born	London, England
Job	Mathematician

The Colossus was the world's first electronic computer and was used by code-breakers during the Second World War. The Colossus was enormous, but it wasn't as powerful as the cheapest home computer you can buy today.

FLYING FACT

BUZZ OFF!

The first computer 'bug' was a moth that got inside the circuits of an early computer and caused an error. This is why computer errors have been called bugs ever since!

Personal computers were cheap enough for ordinary people to buy and use at home.

16 QUIZ The first computer ✱✱✱ was caused by a moth.

It wasn't until the 1960s that computers started to get smaller, when the microchip had been invented! Microchips made it possible to build a whole computer in a box the size of a cereal packet. In the 1970s, inventors such as Stephen Wozniak and Steven Jobs began to build 'personal' computers that could fit on a desktop. Wozniak and Jobs built the first Apple Computer in Jobs' parents' garage!

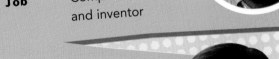

Stephen Wozniak

Born 1950, San Jose, California, USA

Job Computer designer and inventor

Steven Jobs

Born 1955, Los Altos, California, USA

Job Computer designer and businessman

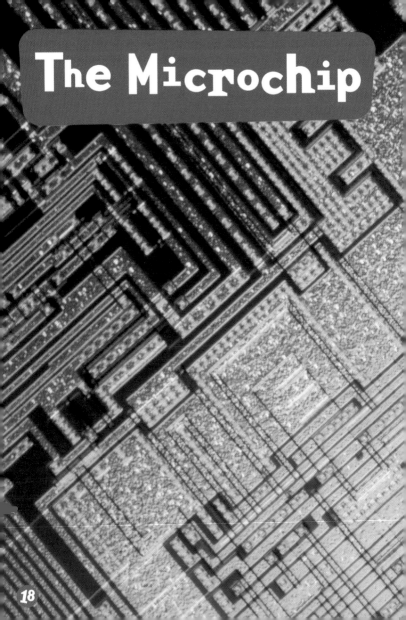

The Microchip

The electric circuits on a microchip are so tiny, you can only see them through a microscope! Microchips are so small that we don't notice that they are all around us! They are in our computers, printers and telephones, but also in cars, stereos, microwaves and cameras. Basically anything that uses electricity these days probably has a microchip in it.

19

The Internet

Computers have created an **information revolution**. By following different programs (lists of instructions), the same computer can handle any kind of information, from numbers and letters, to sounds, pictures and video images. Many jobs that were once done by people are now down by computerised machines.

Police computers hold information on criminals such as photographs and fingerprints.

Then in 1965, two computers, one in Massachusetts, USA and the other in California, USA, were linked by telephone network for the first time. Communication was slow, and there were a lot of errors, but it worked! Companies and government departments started to make their own computer networks. But because different kinds of computer used different codes to send information, one network could not always talk to another.

A network is a set of things things linked together ...

... In 1973, Bob Kahn and Vinton Cerf invented a 'network of networks'. They wanted a way for all kinds of computers to swap information, and in 1983 their ideas were put into practice – the Internet was born!

Robert Kahn

Born   1938, Brooklyn, New York, USA

Job   Computer engineer

Vinton Cerf

Born   1943, New Haven, Connecticut, USA

Job   Computer engineer

Today, if you want to connect a home computer to the Internet, you plug it into a telephone line. This links your personal computer to a powerful computer called a server. The server is owned by your Internet service provider and it is your gateway to millions of other computers linked to the Internet around the world.

Let's Get Technical

The Internet is like a giant electronic post office. Just like every house, every computer linked to the Internet has an address. When you send e-mails or request information through the Internet, your computer sends 'packets' of computer data. Each packet carries the 'addresses' of the computer from which it has come and the one to which it is being sent. Special computers called servers and routers read the addresses, and direct the information through the network.

One of the biggest uses for the Internet is delivering e-mail messages. E-mails may be simple text-only messages, or have pictures, sounds and video clips attached.

send attach addres
To: joe@net.com
Cc: sue@blob.co
Subject: meet
Message:
Hi guys,
How's things
on Saturday
at 2 p.m
outside t

See you..

The World Wide Web is a collection of billions of pages of text, pictures, sounds and video clips stored on the Internet. It was invented by Tim Berners-Lee in 1989. The Web was first developed as a way for scientists to share information. It has since grown into a vast library of every kind of information, that anyone can use.

Tim Berners-Lee

Born 1955, London, England

Job Computer program designer and inventor

Is the World Wide Web the same thing as the
Internet? No! The Internet is all the computers,
wires, optical fibres and radio links that carry
information (e-mail and web pages) around the
world. The World Wide Web is a library of linked
pages of information stored on the Internet.

The first web pages were just text. Some of the text was printed in blue and underlined. These were the 'hyperlinks'. By selecting this text, you could jump to another web page with related information. Then, in 1993, Marc Andreessen invented a 'browser' program that showed text and pictures on the same page. His program used a mouse to select links by pointing and clicking, and made browsing the Web quicker and easier.

Marc Andreessen

Born   1971, Cedar Falls, Iowa, USA

Job   Computer program designer and inventor

There are many search engines today. And many of them search many **other** search engines for the information you need!

Searching for particular information on the Web is made easier by special programs called search engines. Google, for example, makes a list of all the web pages on the Internet. If you enter keywords such as 'Internet history' or 'Tim Berners-Lee', the search engine displays a list of relevant web pages.

You can already do amazing things on the Internet.

- You can connect to a webcam to see what the weather is like in New York at this moment (www.earthcam.com/usa/newyork/timessquare).

- You can check the time on Big Ben's clock (www.camvista.com/england/london/bigben.php3).

But how will the Internet change in the future?

? All forms of entertainment will come through the Internet, from TV and films, to live sports events, concerts and interactive games.

? Internet schools will teach pupils all over the world.

? New cars will be linked to the Internet. The garage will be able to check if a car is working properly no matter where it is.

? Even household appliances will be connected to the Internet. Your fridge might automatically order milk and eggs from the supermarket when you are running low!

Need a rest after all that surfing? Not just yet! Did you get the answers to the quiz questions? Now, juggle with the first letters of all three answers to make a word mentioned in this book.

Juggle with the first letters EBW and you get WEB ...
WORLD WIDE!